Grandee and Her Silly Alphabet

Written by Dede Barr Dunst

Illustrated by Tami Boyce

ISBN: 979-8-35095-525-5

Dedication

Dedicated to my three granddaughters:

Allie — "Grandee and Her Silly Birds"

Emma — "Grandee and Her Silly Week"

Madelyn — "Grandee and Her Silly Alphabet"

About the Author

Dede Barr Dunst is an educator who spent 35 years in the field of early childhood education in the community college systems in North and South Carolina. She graduated from Charlotte Country Day School, and she holds a bachelor's degree in elementary education from Queen's University and a master of education degree from the University of North Carolina-Charlotte. Dede loves inspiring her college students to develop a passion for lifelong learning on their way to becoming early childhood professionals. Dede lives in the Lake Norman area, near Charlotte, N.C. She has a son, a daughter-in-law, and three granddaughters, whose love of books and reading together inspired Dede to write books for children. Dede is retired and enjoys travel, reading, and spending time with her family. ***Grandee and Her Silly Alphabet*** is Dede's third book for young children. To contact Dede, you can email her at nancyconsulting983@gmail.com.

Author photo credit: Rebekah Marie Richardson

About the Illustrator

Tami Boyce is an illustrator and graphic designer based out of Charleston, South Carolina. Believing that the world could use some more levity, Tami pulls artistic inspiration from both her humor and her heart. Her hopes are that while viewing her work, you see something that relates to you, touches your heart, or brings a smile to your face. To see more of her artwork, visit tamiboyce.com.

Facts About Grandee:

Grandee lives on Kangaroo Lane in North Carolina. Grandee drives a new, black Googa car.

Grandee has three granddaughters: Dallie, Demma, and Dadelyn.

Grandee has a son, James. His wife is Lynn.

Grandee's real name is Dede and her mom's name is Gran.

That's how her grandmother name became Grandee!

Let's Read the Alphabet!

Airplane

Blue Jay

Cardinal

Dd
Dog

Elephant

Frog

Gg
Grandee's
Granddaughters

Hh
Helmet

Ii
Ice Cream

Jj
Jar

Kk
Kite

Ll
Ladder

Mm
Monkey

Nn
Necklace

Octopus

Pp
Penguin

Qq
Queen

Rainbow

Ss
Sheep

Tt
Tree

Unicorn

Vv
Violin

Ww
Whale

Xx
Xylophone

Y y
Yo Yo

Zz
Zebra